THE LAW OF LOYALTY

by
LONNIE KEENE
Edited by
KHALILA HAYDEN

Copyright © 2012 Publisher Name
All rights reserved.
ISBN: 1479104612
ISBN 13: 9781479104611

TABLE OF CONTENTS

Foreword .... Dr. David Ireland

Acknowledgements .... Pastor Lonnie Keene

Chapter One......................... I Pledge Allegiance

Chapter Two ....Follow the Leader

Chapter Three .... Loyalty and Relationships

Chapter Four .... The Loyalty Test

Chapter Five ....The Loyalty of God

Chapter Six .... Paths, Places, and People

Chapter Seven .... Take One for the Team

Chapter Eight ...Inspirational Quotes on Loyalty

FOREWORD

By Dr. David Ireland
Founder & Senior Pastor of Christ Church

This book contains priceless gems — rare truths that contemporary Christ-followers must embrace in order to model authentic Christianity. *The Law of Loyalty* calls us back to our biblical roots of loyalty, love, honor, and serving — essential character traits that must be found in disciples of Jesus Christ. Admittedly, it's hard to find someone worthy of your loyalty nowadays; yet you cannot abandon the search. We are commanded to be loyal! Hebrews 13:17 says: "Be responsive to your pastoral leaders. Listen to their counsel. They are alert to the condition of your lives and work under the strict supervision of God. Contribute to the joy of their leadership, not its drudgery. Why would you want to make things harder for them?"

The law of loyalty is seen in how we deal with the people God has placed in our lives. This includes our spiritual leaders. Loyalty is not blind obedience. Blind obedience to a fellow human being is cultish and dangerous. Biblical loyalty is emotionally and spiritually healthy. The one receiving your loyalty should be humbled by this demonstration of honor. Conversely, the one showing loyalty is eager to carry out these finer points of Christian character as a reflection of their devotion to Christ.

Jesus was not afraid to demonstrate loyalty to His followers. When He announced the coming of the Holy Spirit, He was securing the disciples' hopes, dreams, and longings for the transformation of their generation. The Lord's words were: "And I will ask the Father, and he will give you another Counselor to be with you forever — the Spirit of truth ... I will not leave you as orphans" (John 14:16, 18a). These words conveyed a sincere commitment to their continued development and tutelage by readying them to meet the Holy Spirit.

Pastor Keene embodies the message of loyalty. He writes from his knowledge and his experience with God ... and with people. Through *The Law of Loyalty,* Pastor Keene will take you on a journey. At times, the ride will be smooth and easy; learning will be effortless. Yet, at other times the ride will be bumpy. You will be confronted by the Holy Spirit so that full submission to the truth of loyalty can be wholeheartedly embraced. My counsel to you is: Enjoy the ride — all of it.

David D. Ireland, Ph.D., Senior Pastor and Author

The Skin You Live In

ACKNOWLEDGEMENTS

I would like to thank my Lord and Savior Jesus Christ for His grace to help me write this book. I would also like to say a special thank you to the love of my life, my wife Tracy. Thanks for all of your help in seeing that the day-to-day operations of the church run efficiently and effectively, and for your support and encouragement in this endeavor.

To my three sons, Deven, Isaiah, and Jeremiah: Thanks for making my experience as a parent one that I am Godly proud of. You guys are an inspiration to me.

To my parents, Fred and Brenda Keene: Thank you for your unconditional love throughout my life's journey. And to my spiritual father Dr. David Ireland: Thank you for the wisdom you share and for pointing me to my highest potential as a pastor.

I also want to say a special thanks to Kingdom Christian Center, where I'm privileged to pastor. I have learned so much about God, life and myself through the rich relationships I have developed with you. I have been blessed and favored of God to have so many loyal people by my side, which has given me the insight to write this book.

CHAPTER 1

I Pledge Allegiance

Psalm 50:4-5 (The Message Bible)

He summons heaven and earth as a jury, he's taking his people to court, round up my saints who swore on the Bible their loyalty to me.

Loyal = Faithful to law; upholding the lawful authority; faithful and true to the

lawful government; faithful to the prince or sovereign to whom one is subject; unswerving in allegiance.

I remember when I was young, before class would begin in school, we would say the Pledge of Allegiance. *"I pledge allegiance to the flag of the United States of America, and to the republic for which it stands, one nation under God, indivisible, with liberty and justice for all."*

According to our national flag code, the United States flag should be displayed daily on or near the main administration building of every public institution. In other words, displaying the US flag in public institutions is a law and it is a statement of loyalty to our government. On this basis, I've entitled this book the ***Law of Loyalty.***

Laws are in motion all around us, including the law of gravity, the law of lift, the law of attraction, the law of sympathetic resonance, the law of love, the law of faith, and the law of seedtime and harvest. Let's learn about the Law of Loyalty.

The mafia, street gangs, and fraternities pledge their allegiance to their respective organizations. How much more should we pledge our allegiance as Christians?

Here are three things we as Christians should pledge our allegiance to.

1. Pledge your allegiance to God.

In Daniel 3:17-25, you can read the account of the three Hebrew boys – Shadrach, Meshach and Abednego. King Nebuchadnezzar decreed that everyone in the kingdom had to bow down and worship a giant golden image. Whoever refused to worship the image was to be thrown into the burning fiery furnace.

But Shadrach, Meshach and Abednego didn't surrender to the king's law. They had already pledged their allegiance to God. Word of the three Hebrews rebellion against the king's decree got back to the king and he told them to either worship the golden image or be burned alive in a fiery furnace. But because of their allegiance, God delivered them.

In Daniel 6:1-10, King Darius signed a decree banning prayer. But the Bible says Daniel kept praying three times a day in spite of the decree. As a punishment, the king threw him into the lion's den. The king came back the next day expecting Daniel to be dead. But God had stopped the mouths of the lions because Daniel had pledged his allegiance to God. *As we can see, attacks are assigned to alter our allegiance.*

Some Bible scholars believe that in the end times people will have to receive the mark of the beast – also known as 666 – in their bodies to buy or sell things or even to get food. They believe people won't be able to do anything without that mark. Its sole purpose will be to get people to surrender their allegiance to God and obey the world's system. This is another attack by the anti-Christ to alter our allegiance.

Have you seen the movie *The Avengers*? In it, a villain named Loki gets into a fight with the Incredible Hulk. In the midst of the fight, he tells the Hulk, "I'm a god!" Loki wanted the Hulk's allegiance. But the Hulk just pulverized him. When things attack you and try to alter your allegiance, God gets angry. He becomes like the Hulk in your life and becomes your avenger. That's because you have pledged your allegiance to Him.

In Exodus 32, Moses went up into Mount Sinai to talk with God, but because the children of Israel thought he was gone too long, they asked Aaron the priest to make them a god to worship, and it displeased the Lord. When Moses came down from the mount, he asked the people a question to determine their allegiance. He asked, "Who is on God's side? Let him come unto me." As Christians we ought to pledge our allegiance to God.

2. Pledge your allegiance to a man of God.

In Samuel 14:1-13, Jonathan's armor bearer pledged his allegiance to his man of God. He told Jonathan, *do all that is in thy heart, I am with you according to thine heart.* Your pastor has an assignment, and an anointing on his life to assist you in living your best life, but it requires your allegiance.

In ministry over the years, I've heard Christians in the church say, "I'm not doing what man says. I'm only doing what God says." That's not true. Your employer tells you what time to come to work. The IRS tells you to file your taxes by April 15th. The dentist tells you to open your mouth wide while he comes at you with sharp, jagged tools in his hand. You don't even know him. He could be Jeffrey Dahmer on crack! Your doctor tells you to take off all your clothes. If you're a man who needs a prostate exam, he first reaches for lubricating cream, slides on a glove, tells you to bend over and you do it!

In the Gospel of John 2, the people at the wedding in Cana ran out of wine. Jesus happened to be at the wedding and Mary said, concerning Jesus, *whatever he tells you to do, do it.* In other words, when you start running out of ideas, answers, patience, time, or money, do what your man of God tells you to do, and watch water be turned into wine in your life.

Your allegiance to him should be based on his character, integrity, and reputation,

The spiritual covering for the church I pastor is Dr. David Ireland who pastors Christ Church in Rockaway, New Jersey. I'll never forget what he said when he accepted my request to be the spiritual covering for our ministry. He said that he and his wife Marlinda would live the kind of life that is above reproach, the kind of life that my wife Tracy and I and the Kingdom Christian Center (KCC) congregation could be proud of. Because of the assignment and anointing on his life to help me be the best pastor I can be, I do what he tells me to do.

3. Pledge your allegiance to the Church of God

Acts 11:21-26

And the hand of the Lord was with them: and a great number believed, and turned unto the Lord. 22 Then tidings of these things came unto the ears of the church which was in Jerusalem: and they sent forth Barnabas, that he should go as far as Antioch. 23 Who, when he came, and had seen the grace of God, was glad, and exhorted them all, that with purpose of heart they would cleave unto the Lord. 24 For he was a good man, and full of the Holy Ghost and of faith: and much people was added unto the Lord. 25 Then departed Barnabas to Tarsus, for to seek Saul: 26 And when he had found him, he brought him unto Antioch. And it came to pass, that a whole year they assembled themselves with the church, and taught much people. And the disciples were called Christians first in Antioch.

In verses 21, 23, and 24, it describes how those who believed were added to the Lord. In verse 26, it describes how they assembled themselves to the church. Let me explain. I love the game of basketball. There have been times when a player makes a great move and the crowd goes bonkers, but the move isn't a finished success if he misses the layup. It's a great move to be added unto the Lord, as we see in verses 21, 23 and 24, but that move isn't a finished success if you leave out verse 26 which says to assemble yourself to the Church.

How do we pledge our allegiance to the Church?

a. We give our time.

At my church, we put out a yearly calendar of church events in January and ask our members to plan their lives around what's going on at the church. Planning makes us considerate of our members' other obligations and it makes our members conscious of the importance of coming to church.

Think about it. You have 24 hours in a day and seven days in a week, which adds up to 168 hours a week. People generally work eight hours a day five days a week, which adds up to 40 hours a week. Subtract the 40 hours a week from the 168 hours that you're allotted and that leaves you with 128 hours a week. People generally sleep eight hours a night seven nights a week, which adds up to 56 hours a week. Subtract the 56 hours a week from the 128 hours you have left and that leaves you with 72 hours a week. People generally spend about 10 hours a week running errands and doing chores. Take those 10 hours a week and subtract them from the 72 hours you have left and that leaves you with 62 hours a week to do whatever you want to do. At KCC, we have service for about two hours on Sunday and one hour on Wednesday. That's three hours a week. Now with 62 hours a week to do whatever you want to do, you mean to tell me you can't give the church three of those hours? That's not even a tithe of our time!

Kingdom Christian Center is located in Columbus, Ohio. We have a wonderful married couple who visited our church from Pittsburgh. One Sunday the wife was in Columbus visiting her family and she ended up coming to our church. She loved it so much that she joined. She went back to Pittsburgh and told her husband about us. He came and loved it so much that he joined. Then they began to drive from Pittsburgh to Columbus three hours one way every Sunday for five years until God opened a door for both of them to be relocated. Now they live in Columbus and give their time to the church. Is that not a testimony of loyalty and allegiance to the Church? I have members who live around the corner who aren't here every Sunday.

b. We give our talent.

God has given us talents, gifts, and abilities to serve the Church.

When you serve in the Church it allows you to express your potential.

Never complain that serving is like work because without work you couldn't express your potential. The Bible tells us in Ephesians 4:11-12 that God gave us gifts so they could be used in the church *for the perfecting of the saints and the work of the ministry*. So never complain that serving in the house of God is like work! Ministry is work, but that's the way it's supposed to be. Without work you couldn't express your potential!

When you serve in the Church it allows you to fulfill a portion of your purpose.

Why did I say just a portion? As a pastor I understand, that our members' lives aren't totally consumed with church 24 hours a day, seven days a week. There are some other assignments and dreams that God has placed in their hearts that are outside of the church that help them fulfill their purpose. But there's a great portion of their purpose that can ONLY be fulfilled in the church. At KCC, our purpose is to inspire people to live a better quality of life through Jesus Christ. For example, in October 2011 we gave away 400 pairs of brand new shoes to people in need. We used our resources to fulfill our purpose to show people that there is a better quality of life!

When you serve in the Church it allows you to get plugged in.

I call it the power of attachment. I remember every night I used to plug my old iPhone into the charger at home, but the battery would die not long after. Then I would plug it in at my office and it would keep its charge. When I would plug it in at home, the phone would lose its charge again. This went on for days. One morning when I was going to unplug my phone, I noticed that I had not been using my attachment; it was my wife's attachment. It looked like mine, but because I was trying to charge my phone using the wrong attachment it wasn't getting the power it needed. When you're attached to the wrong people, places and things, you can't figure out why you feel so drained in your life because you don't have an understanding of the power of attachments. But when you get attached to the Church it will charge you and it will change you. It will give you cathectic energy – not just spiritual energy, not just physical energy, but mental energy. In other words, you'll start gaining what the older saints called having a mind to serve Christ.

When you serve in the Church it allows you to assist your pastor.

In Exodus 17, while the children of Israel fought the Amelkites, Aaron and Hur held Moses' hands up. When Joshua and the men saw Moses hands begin to fall, they started losing the fight. But when they could see Moses hands lifted, they were successful in battle. If your leader looks tired and drained, so goes the people under him. But if your leader looks strong, healthy, energized and up for the fight, then what's in the leader will get in you! If al-Qaeda can assist Osama bin Laden, if the Crips and Bloods can assist the OG, if Jonathan's armor bearer can assist Jonathan, then surely you can assist your pastor.

c. We give our treasure.

Malachi 3:10 says, *Bring ye the tithes into the storehouse, that there may be meat in mine house, and prove me now herewith, saith the Lord of hosts, if I will not open you the windows of heaven and pour you out a blessing.*

Many churches receive financial pledges from their partners and members to help fulfill the vision of that church. Giving tithes and offerings is another way to pledge your allegiance to your church. Malachi 3:10 says that when you tithe God opens the windows of heaven and pours you out a blessing. Blessing is a declaration of divine favor; that which promotes prosperity and welfare; a benediction. The blessing speaks to the end of a thing. For example, I told you I love the game of basketball. Most kids put all their hope in being on the starting five, but in basketball it's not who starts the game, it's who finishes the game. You may not have started the game strong, but I believe you're going to finish the game strong! I prophesy a finishing grace over your life right now in Jesus' name!

The Bible says looking unto Jesus who is the author and finisher of our faith. The Bible says *being confident of this very thing that he which hath begun a good work in you will finish it until the day of Jesus Christ.* Paul said *I fought a good fight; I finished my course.* I believe you will finish strong as a result of your loyalty and pledging your allegiance.

I pledge allegiance to the church and to the kingdom for which it stands one church under God, indivisible with liberty and justice and favor and blessing and peace and prosperity and goodness and glory for all!

CHAPTER 2

Follow the Leader

Hebrews 13:7 (King James Version)

Remember them which have the rule over you, who have spoken unto you the word of God: whose faith follow, considering the end of their conversation.

Hebrews 13:7 (Amplified Bible)

Remember your leaders and superiors in authority [for it was they] who brought to you the Word of God. Observe attentively and consider their manner of living (the outcome of their well-spent lives) and imitate their faith (their conviction that God exists and is the Creator and Ruler of all things, the Provider and Bestower of eternal salvation through Christ, and their leaning of the entire human personality on God in absolute trust and confidence in His power, wisdom, and goodness).

Growing up, I played a game called follow the leader. First a leader or the head of the line would be chosen. Then the children would all line up behind the leader. The leader would move around and all the children would have to mimic or imitate the leader's actions. Any player who failed to do what the leader did was out of the game. The last person standing other than the leader then became the new leader.

I believe God wants to raise up new leaders in politics, business, and the church, but the prerequisite to becoming a leader is learning how to become a follower. We teach our children to be leaders and not followers, and we do them a disservice when we do. There is absolutely no way to become a good leader, if you haven't first become a great follower. So what we need to teach them is what to look for in a leader before they follow.

Many people look for gifts, charisma, great communicators. I agree these are great attributes in a leader, but in Hebrews 13:7 (Amplified Bible) it says *observe attentively and consider their manner of living (the outcome of their well-spent lives).* How would you like to have a physical trainer who is obese, a financial adviser who is broke, a lawyer who is in prison or a dentist who has halitosis and gum disease? When someone tries to sell me something, my first question is, "Do you use it?" What I want to know is, "Are you applying what you're offering?" I believe leaders who are worthy of our loyalty have the outcome of a well spent life. These aren't perfect men and women, or problem-free men and women. But they are men and women who have a pure heart before the Lord.

In Bishop Tudor Bismark's book *The Spirit of Honor,* he says loyalty produces loyalty. In other words, loyalty doesn't start with followers. Loyalty starts with leaders. Let me use a principle that I believe applies to loyalty. When God gave Adam a woman, he didn't go to the dust of the ground to make her. He reached inside Adam, took a rib, and made Eve. In other words, Adam didn't get what he wanted as much as he got what he was. I've had the opportunity to teach in all types of churches, and I've observed this principle in operation. If the leader wore stylish suits and Stacy Adam shoes, many of the followers did also. If the leader wore khakis and a polo shirt, many of the followers did also. If the leader was overweight, many of the followers were also. If the leader was broke, many of the followers were also. You don't produce what you want, you produce what you are. That takes me back to Bishop Tudor Bismark's statement: Loyalty produces loyalty.

Now there's a difference between loyalty and faithfulness. Sometimes people think that because they're faithful they're loyal too. But that's not true. Faithful is what you do, but loyalty is why you do it. So you can be faithful and doing the right things, but doing them for the wrong reasons. In that case, you're faithful, not loyal. Loyalty is birthed out of love. Loyalty means to do the right thing even up against opposition. A good leader is going to do what's best for you whether you like it or not. For example, if a leader were to withhold the truth from you just to make you happy, he or she wouldn't be being loyal to you.

Let's look at three things that make people want to follow the leader.

Matthew 4:19, 20

And he saith unto them, Follow me, and I will make you fishers of men. And they straightway left their nets, and followed him.

1. A leader's promise creates a follower's loyalty.

Hebrews 6:12 says, *be not slothful, but followers of them who through faith and patience inherit the promises.* Jesus made a promise to potential followers; he said follow me and I'll make you fishers of men. How do major corporations create loyal customers or followers? They make a promise. Lexus' promise is "extraordinary customer satisfaction." Hilton hotels promise "to put back a little of what life takes out." Wal-Mart promises that you'll "Save money. Live better." At Kingdom Christian Center

Church, we promise "to inspire people to live a better quality of life through Jesus Christ."

If you want to create loyalty in your home as a family leader, if you want to create loyalty in your customers as a business leader, if you want to create loyalty in your constituents as a political leader, and if you want to create loyalty in your members as a church leader, then you must know what you promise.

Let's take a look at another attribute that makes people want to follow the leader.

John 9:19-25

And they asked them, saying, Is this your son, who ye say was born blind? how then doth he now see? His parents answered them and said, We know that this is our son, and that he was born blind: But by what means he now seeth, we know

not; or who hath opened his eyes, we know not: he is of age; ask him: he shall speak for himself.

These words spake his parents, because they feared the Jews: for the Jews had agreed already, that if any man did confess that he was Christ, he should be put out of the synagogue. Therefore said his parents, He is of age; ask him. Then again called they the man that was blind, and said unto him, Give God the praise: we know that this man is a sinner. He answered and said, Whether he be a sinner or no, I know not: one thing I know, that, whereas I was blind, now I see.

2. A leader's problem-solving abilities create a follower's loyalty.

To acknowledge Jesus as the Christ could have had this young man thrown out of the synagogue. His parents understood that; that's why the scripture says, *they feared the Jews.* They didn't want to be put out of the synagogue so instead of answering the Jews they told them to go talk to their son themselves. See, Jesus didn't help the parents, he helped the son. So the parents had no allegiance to Jesus and because of that they didn't want to stand up against the religious order of the day. The Jews also accused Jesus of being a sinner, but this young man's loyalty wouldn't allow him to chime in with such allegations because Jesus had solved a problem for him.

A great example of this is found in the movie the *Rise of the Planet of the Apes.* In the movie, a young ape named Caesar was somewhat of a house pet to his owner. After an innocent incident that was misunderstood, Caesar was taken from his owner and placed in a shelter with other apes. This shelter environment was like a prison. The first time Caesar was put into the public population, he was bullied by an ape that seemed to run all the other apes, while this was going on Caesar noticed a huge, fierce ape that was locked up and kept in isolation from the other apes. Because of Caesar's intelligence, he stole the keeper's key, and one evening while all the other apes were asleep he unlocked the cell that held this huge, fierce ape.

The ape couldn't believe that his cell was open. He took a moment and then charged out after Caesar. Caesar was able to avoid his wrath by outrunning him. After a few seconds, the ape stopped and starred at Caesar. Caesar then pulled out a cookie and gave it to this huge, fierce ape and in doing so he captured the ape's loyalty. Not only had Caesar freed the ape, Caesar had fed him too. The next time Caesar was let into the public population with all the other apes that same ape that bullied him the first time came after him again, but this time Caesar had unlocked the cell that held the huge, fierce ape. That ape came out and stood up for Caesar, suggesting to the bully ape, and all the other apes that Caesar was now the new leader of all the apes. In other words, Caesar gained this huge, fierce ape's loyalty because he solved a problem for him. A leader's problem-solving abilities create a follower's loyalty!

If you read 2 Samuel 15:2-6, you'll see that King David's son Absalom understood this too. While King David was inside the palace taking care of kingdom business, Absalom positioned himself at the gate of the city. When the followers of David would come to the palace seeking answers to problems, Absalom would catch the people before they entered and tell them the king hadn't appointed anyone to give them answers that day. Then he would tell them, "Oh, if I was the judge in Israel, I would do you justice."

What Absalom was telling the people was, "If I was king I could solve your problems." The Bible said Absalom began to steal the hearts of the people from King David, as he did this. He understood if he could usurp King David's authority and solve the people's problems before they got to King David, he could alter their allegiance and cause them to be loyal to him and that's exactly what he did. That's why you must remember, as a member of your church, you are simply an extension of your pastor. No matter what you're doing in your church's various ministries, remember you're doing it in your pastor's anointing. Don't try to steal people's hearts unto yourself; always point them back to your pastor.

In 1 Samuel 22, David went down to the cave of Adullam and 400 men followed him there. They were distressed, discontented, and in debt and they needed answers. They spent time in the cave with David and he began to solve their problems. By the time the men left, they became known as mighty men. Because David solved their problems, he created loyalty among the people.

In another passage in the Bible, Jesus arrives at a house to find the disciples standing outside. He asked them why they hadn't gone in. The disciples told him they hadn't gone in because no one was there to wash their feet. Jesus took a towel and a basin and began to wash the disciples' feet. Peter told Jesus to stop, saying "Oh no Lord you're too important to do such a thing." But Jesus told him *unless I wash your feet you won't have any part with me.* In others words, Jesus was saying if I don't serve you, wash you up and turn some things around in your life, you won't be loyal to me.

This doesn't mean you won't have bumps in the road in your walk of loyalty. Remember Peter denied Christ. But when loyalty is really in your heart, it causes you to bounce back. Peter did the same thing Judas did. They both denied and betrayed Jesus. But why wasn't Judas able to bounce back? It's because Jesus never solved a problem for him. Judas wanted Jesus to overthrow the Roman government. But that wasn't Jesus' mission. Because He didn't solve Judas' "problem" with the Roman government, Jesus never gained Judas' loyalty.

John 6:63-68

It is the spirit that quickeneth; the flesh profiteth nothing: the words that speak unto you, they are spirit, and they are life. But there are some of you that believe not. For Jesus knew from the beginning who they were that believed not, and who should betray him. And he said, Therefore said I unto you, that no man can come unto me, except it were given unto him of my Father. From that time many of his disciples went back, and walked no more with him. Then said Jesus unto the twelve, Will ye also go away? Then Simon Peter answered him, Lord, to whom shall we go? thou hast the words of eternal life.

3. A leader's preaching creates a follower's loyalty.

Loyalty refuses to leave a leader who has a word that is life giving. For example, Elisha refused to leave Elijah because Elijah's words were so life giving. Elijah said unto Elisha *tarry here for the Lord hath sent me to Bethel, Jericho and Jordan* and Elisha said *I will not leave thee.* He followed the leader.

Ruth refused to leave Naomi because Naomi's words were so life giving. Naomi told Ruth to go home to her people but Ruth said, *Intreat me not to leave thee, or to return from following after thee: for whither thou goest, I will go; and where thou lodgest, I will lodge: thy people shall be my people, and thy God my God.* She followed the leader! Peter refused to leave Jesus because Jesus' words were so life giving. Jesus said my words are spirit and they are life. Jesus asked Peter will you go also, and Peter said *to whom shall we go? Thou hast the words of eternal life.* Peter followed the leader!

What's the common thread through these three stories? **There's always great manifestation for those who are willing to stick in there**

and follow the leader. Because Elisha kept following Elijah, he ended up receiving a double portion of Elijah's anointing. Because Ruth continued to follow her leader Naomi, she ended up meeting a wealthy man named Boaz who became her husband. Peter told Jesus we've left everything to follow you. But Jesus said for any man who has left fathers, mothers, houses, and lands for my sake and the gospel's sake, there's going to be some manifestation coming back unto him. So there's manifestation for those who keep following the leader! My question is: Are you willing to follow the leader? Are you willing to follow your leader into the blessed life, into a blessed marriage, into a wonderful relationship with the Lord, into communion with the Holy Spirit, into increase, into manifestation? Are you willing to follow your leader into momentum?

The next leaders of this generation keep following the leader! Good preaching and good training through the Word of God that is life giving creates a follower's loyalty! I'm talking about the kind of teaching that infuses your spirit and causes life to be birthed and causes you to want to change for the better! That's the kind of preaching that creates loyalty!

Paul said it best, *"Follow me as I follow Christ."* Paul wasn't a god. He was a man of God and he understood that it's beneficial for people to follow good leaders as they follow Christ.

CHAPTER 3

Loyalty and Relationships

Proverbs 17:17 *A friend loveth at all times and a brother is born for adversity.*

I believe that relationships are tremendous gifts from God. There is nothing more valuable than a God-intended relationship. The relationship I have with my wife Tracy, my children Deven, Isaiah, and Jeremiah, my church and friends are the most important things in my life. That's because I understand that relationships can refresh us, refine us, reward us, and are resources for us.

Researchers recently conducted a study at Northwestern University that found that a high percentage of relationships are successful because of an understanding of loyalty.

Loyalty is what makes marriages affair-proof. Loyalty is what stops church splits. Loyalty is what keeps employees loyal to their employer. Loyalty is what causes two people to stay forever friends. Loyalty is the link to strong relationships. To understand how loyalty impacts relationships, let's look at satan's mistake.

Isaiah 14:12-15

How art thou fallen from heaven, O Lucifer, son of the morning! how art thou cut down to the ground, which didst weaken the nations! 13 For thou hast said in thine heart, I will ascend into heaven, I will exalt my throne above the stars of God: I will sit also upon the mount of the congregation, in the sides of the north: 14 I will ascend above the heights of the clouds; I will be like the most High. 15 Yet thou shalt be brought down to hell, to the sides of the pit.

Remember loyalty means: Faithful to law; upholding the lawful authority; faithful and true to the lawful government; faithful to the prince or sovereign to whom one is subject; unswerving in allegiance.

Isaiah 14 is a perfect example of how Lucifer (the devil), lacked loyalty and as a result it ruined his relationship with God. He learned firsthand that a lack of loyalty has the ability to ruin relationships. After he was thrown out of heaven, the first place he showed up was in the Garden of Eden in the form of a serpent attacking Adam and Eve's loyalty.

Genesis 3:1-5

Now the serpent was more subtil than any beast of the field which the

Lord God had made. And he said unto the woman, Yea, hath God said, Ye shall not eat of every tree of the garden? 2 And the woman said unto the serpent, We may eat of the

fruit of the trees of the garden: 3 But of the fruit of the tree which is in the midst of the garden, God hath said, Ye shall not eat of it, neither shall ye touch it, lest ye die. 4 And the serpent said unto the woman, Ye shall not surely die: 5 For God doth know that in the day ye eat thereof, then your eyes shall be opened, and ye shall be as gods, knowing good and evil.

The serpent (the devil), attacked Adam and Eve's loyalty to God and in doing so he was able to ruin their relationship with God. In the rest of this chapter, I want to reveal three things that the devil uses to attack loyalty and ruin relationships, and how we can overcome these attacks, and experience healthy, long-lasting relationships.

The first thing he uses is: 1. Insinuation

Insinuation means to introduce gently or slowly; to introduce artfully; to infuse gently; to instill; to hint. As John Locke, the famous British philosopher, once said, "All the art of rhetoric, besides order and clearness, are for nothing else but to insinuate wrong ideas, move the passions, and thereby mislead the judgment."

Genesis 3:1

Now the serpent was more subtil than any beast of the field which the Lord God had made. And he said unto the woman, Yea, hath God said, Ye shall not eat of every tree of the garden?

He's trying to introduce wrong ideas about God. Insinuation introduces wrong ideas about the person you're loyal to. Adam and Eve should have asked the serpent, "What are you insinuating?" A man may say to a married woman, "If you weren't married ..." What is he insinuating? A woman may say to a married man, "Your wife is lucky to have you." What is she insinuating? A church member may say to another church member, "What did you think of Pastor's message today?" What is that person insinuating?

Insinuation is artful articulation with an agenda and if you allow enough insinuation inside you, it will have you questioning your loyalty to a relationship.

The second thing the enemy uses is: 2. Injustice

2 Samuel 15:2-4

And Absalom rose up early, and stood beside the way of the gate: and it was so, that when any man that had a controversy came to the king for judgment, then Absalom called unto him, and said, Of what city art thou? And he said, Thy servant is of one of the tribes of Israel. 3 And Absalom said unto him,

See, thy matters are good and right; but there is no man deputed of the king to hear thee. 4 Absalom said moreover, Oh that I were made judge in the land, that every man which hath any suit or cause might come unto me, and I would do him justice!

If you read the rest of this story, you'll see that Absalom stole the hearts of the men from King David by insinuating that they were suffering from an injustice.

There are still some African Americans who struggle with loyalty to this country because of slavery, which was a horrible injustice. While I can certainly understand those feelings, I also understand that through the sovereignty and purpose of God injustice can serve as a vehicle to increase. African Americans now have the opportunity to live in the greatest nation on Earth.

Joseph suffered a great injustice from his brothers, but he refused to allow it to affect his loyalty toward them. He said *ye thought evil against me, but God meant it unto good* (Genesis 50:20). The injustice he suffered became a vehicle to his increase. You may be suffering from an injustice in your family, on your job, with your co-workers, in the church, but God told me to tell you, "Don't let it steal your loyalty. The injustice is about to become a vehicle to your increase!"

The third thing he uses is: 3. Injury

Psalm 55:12-14

For it was not an enemy that reproached me; then I could have borne it: neither was it he that hated me that did magnify himself against me; then I would have hid myself from him: 13 But it was thou, a man mine equal, my guide, and mine acquaintance. 14 We took sweet counsel together, and walked unto the house of God in company.

The acquaintance King David is talking about here is a man named Ahithophel, who was his counselor – the one David shared his secrets with, the one to whom he directed all of his affairs, the one he walked into the house of God with. David said if it was an enemy "*I could have borne it,*" suggesting that since it was someone close to him it caused injury.

When I was just a boy, I had a German shepherd that I loved and he loved me. One day as I was coming home from school, I witnessed my dog get hit by a car. Afterwards, he hobbled up and into the corner of our porch. As I approached him to care for him and to see if he was ok, he growled at me as if he was going to bite me if I came any closer. A day later, he ran away and I never saw him again. It's amazing how his injury affected his loyalty to me.

Remember I said that relationships refresh us, refine us, reward us, and are resources for us? When we've been injured relationships are also risks for us. People are like mathematics – you have adders, you have subtractors, you have multipliers, and you have dividers.

So anytime you embark upon a new relationship, you take the risk of the person being an adder, a subtractor, a multiplier, or a divider. People are the problem, but yet people are the answer. So if you keep running away from the problem, you'll never get the answer.

The devil used a person to hurt you. God's going to use a person to heal you! The devil used a man to tear you down. God's going to use a man to build you up! The devil used a father to molest you. God's going to use a father to minister to you! The devil used someone to betray you. God's going to use someone who's got your back! Don't let your pain paralyze you from a God-intended relationship.

A personal trainer in my church once told me that if people are going to be successful at lifting weights they must learn how to push past the pain! When going through physical therapy, you must push past the pain! When a woman gives birth, she must push past the pain!

You may have been betrayed, backstabbed, bamboozled, broken, bruised and left bleeding, but you don't have to let insinuation, injustice or injury stop you from having loyal relationships.

CHAPTER 4

The Loyalty Test

2 Corinthians 9:12, 13 (Amplified Bible)

For the service that the ministering of this fund renders does not only fully supply what is lacking to the saints (God's people), but it also overflows in many [cries of] thanksgiving to God. 13 Because at [your] standing of the test of this ministry, they will glorify God for your loyalty and obedience to the Gospel of Christ which you confess, as well as for your generous-hearted liberality to them and to all [the other needy ones].

Loyalty isn't loyalty, if it isn't put to the test. In chapter one, I talked about gang members pledging their allegiance. Well, let me add that before people can join a gang, they have to go through some type of initiation. It's the same with fraternities and sororities. That initiation is not only a matter of pledging allegiance; it's also putting their loyalty to the test.

Remember when your girlfriend or boyfriend would ask you to call your ex and tell your ex it was all over, while they listened in on another phone? That person was putting your loyalty to the test. How about when your girlfriend said I love you in front of all of your homeboys? What was she doing? She was putting your loyalty to the test. Loyalty isn't loyalty, if it isn't put to the test.

God holds an interesting conversation with satan in the book of Job. During the conversation satan basically tells God he had been roaming the Earth causing havoc in people's lives. God asked him if he had considered his servant Job. Satan said he would have tried but God kept a hedge of protection around Job. Then satan said, *"But put forth thine hand now, and touch all that he hath, and he will curse thee to thy face"* (Job 1:11). After Job went through all the afflictions the enemy put him through, his wife asked him, *Why do you still hold on to your integrity, why don't you curse God and die?* But the Bible says in all this *Job did not sin with his lips* (Job 2:10). It was as if God was putting Job's loyalty to the test.

In Genesis 22, God asked Abraham to sacrifice his only son Isaac. When Abraham was about to go through with what God had asked of him, an angel of the Lord called out from heaven and said, *Lay not thine hand upon the lad, neither do thou any thing unto him: for now I know that thou fearest God, seeing thou hast not withheld thy son, thine only son from me* (Genesis 22:12). It was as if God was putting Abraham's loyalty to the test.

In Matthew 10:37, Jesus said, *He that loveth father or mother more than me is not worthy of me: and he that loveth son or daughter more than me is not worthy of me.* It was as if He was putting believers' loyalty to the test.

In this chapter, I want to talk about some areas where we as Christians will most likely be put to the test and how loyalty isn't loyalty, if it isn't put to the test. I believe you're going to be blessed.

1. The Morality Test

Genesis 39:5-12

And it came to pass from the time that he had made him overseer in his house, and over all that he had, that the Lord blessed the Egyptian's house for

Joseph's sake; and the blessing of the Lord was upon all that he had in the house, and in the field. 6 And he left all that he had in Joseph's hand; and he knew not ought he had, save the bread which he did eat. And Joseph was a goodly person, and well favoured. 7 And it came to pass after these things, that his master's wife cast her eyes upon Joseph; and she said, Lie with me. 8 But he refused, and said unto his master's

wife, Behold, my master wotteth not what is with me in the house, and he hath committed all that he hath to my hand; 9 There is none greater in this house than I; neither hath he kept back any thing from me but thee, because thou art his wife: how then can I do this great wickedness, and sin against God? 10 And it came to pass, as she spake to Joseph day by day, that he hearkened not unto her, to lie by her, or to be with her. 11 And it came to pass about this time, that Joseph went into the house to do his business; and there was none of the men of the house there within. 12 And she caught him by his garment, saying, Lie with me: and he left his garment in her hand, and fled, and got him out.

Joseph had the opportunity to sleep with his master's wife, but because of his loyalty to

Potiphar and his loyalty to God he refused to do so. This passage says when Joseph went into the house to take care of business no one else was in the house. So he had a prime opportunity to get away with what Potiphar's wife wanted. But, like integrity, loyalty means doing the right thing even when no one's looking. Joseph passed the loyalty test because he did the right thing when no one was looking. It's easy for a man to do the right thing when his wife, his boss, or his pastor is looking. But as a pastor, I'm impressed with those who faithfully serve behind the scenes in my church when no one's looking. They're busy copying CDs, cutting fresh fruit, counting money, and cuddling babies when no one's looking. To me that's the model of loyalty.

Too much immorality has been the story lately when it comes to our politicians, and sadly when it comes to many prominent preachers. I once heard Dr. I.V. Hilliard, who pastors a great church in Houston, Texas tell this story. He said one day he was driving with another preacher in Houston. The preacher began to talk about all the beautiful women that Dr. Hilliard had in his church, and asked him why he hadn't slept with any of these fine women. Dr. Hilliard pulled into a nearby corner store. Before he got out of his car to go inside, he reached into his pocket, pulled out a $100 bill and placed it on the dashboard. He then got out and went into the store for a few moments. When Dr. Hilliard got back into his car he noticed the $100 bill was still where he left it on the dashboard. He asked this preacher, "Didn't you see the $100 bill I left here?" The preacher said yes. "Why didn't you take it? Didn't you want it?" Dr. Hilliard asked him.

The preacher said, "Sure I wanted it, but the reason I didn't touch it is because it doesn't belong to me." Dr. Hilliard then said, "That's why I don't mess with any of those beautiful women in my church. It's because they don't belong to me." Thank God Dr. Hilliard passed the morality test. I believe that every man or woman who is going to be blessed will be faced with the morality test.

2. The Money Test

In Joshua 7, after Israel won a battle God told them not to take anything for themselves.

But a man named Achan said, *When I saw among the spoils a goodly Babylonish garment, and two hundred shekels of silver, and a wedge of gold of fifty*

shekels weight, then I coveted them, and took them; and, behold, they are hid in the

earth in the midst of my tent, and the silver under it (Joshua 7:21).There were major consequences to his theft. He failed the money test.

In Mark 10, one man came and asked Jesus, what he had to do to inherit eternal life. Jesus said *One thing thou lackest: go thy way, sell whatsoever thou hast, and give to the poor, and thou shalt have treasure in heaven: and come, take up the cross, and follow me. And he was sad at that saying, and went away grieved: for he had great possessions.* What happened here? This man had more loyalty to his possessions than he had toward the Lord. He failed the money test.

In Acts 5, Ananias and his wife Sapphira sold a possession and kept back part of the price. The Bible says, *His wife also being privy to it, and brought a certain part, and laid it at the apostles' feet. But Peter said, Ananias, why hath Satan filled thine heart to lie to the Holy Ghost, and to keep back part of the price of the land? Whiles it remained, was it not thine own? and after it was sold, was it not in thine own power? why hast thou conceived this thing in thine heart? thou hast not lied unto men, but unto God.* Soon after, his wife came in and did the same thing, and they both fell dead.

What happened? They failed the money test.

Much of the economic downfall that our country is experiencing today is because of major lending institutions that came up with "creative financing" for mortgages – otherwise known as greed. Here we are years later still trying to dig ourselves out because many of these men and women failed the money test.

Recently I paid $20 for four of my family members to go to a basketball game. I gave the person selling the tickets a $100 bill. He in return gave me five $20 bills back as my change. I understand that some people would consider that transaction a blessing, or favor, or the goodness of God, but I considered it a money test. I understand that a $200 or a $2,000 mistake is more tempting than a $20 mistake, but the Bible says, if you can't be faithful (or loyal) over a few things, then you won't be faithful (or loyal) over many things. I was not going to let $20 cause me to fail the money test. I believe God has much more money that He wants me to manage, and I can't allow the love of money or loyalty to money cause me to fail that test.

Let's look at someone else who passed the money test.

In 1 Kings 17, the widow woman in Zarephath passed the money test. There was a famine in the land. But God caused this widow woman to sustain the prophet Elijah. The widow woman had so little food left that she was going to make one last cake for her and her son. Then they were going to eat it and die. But the prophet asked her to give him a little bit first. She only had a little bit! Her loyalty was being tested. She gave him a little bit and God did something miraculous in her home because she didn't fail the money test.

3. The Ministry Test

Loyalty isn't proven when everything is happy, healthy, heavenly and in harmony in ministry. Loyalty is proven when you get hurt in ministry, but you learn how to manage the hurt, bounce back from the hurt and continue to be a great help in ministry. I can't tell you how many people have left churches because they felt as though they had been hurt there. But that's no excuse to leave the church. Those same people were hurt on the job, but they kept going to work. Those same people were hurt in the night club, but they kept going out every Friday. Those same people were hurt in casinos, but they kept gambling their lives away. Many of us know women who kept going back to abusive relationships. Being hurt in the church is no excuse to leave the church.

I'm convinced that many Christians today would have left Jesus' ministry. Jesus told one woman, *It is not meet to take the children's bread, and to cast it to dogs.* That had to hurt, but she kept coming to Jesus. Jesus spit in one man's eyes. That had to be embarrassing, but he didn't run away. Jesus told Peter, *Get thee behind me Satan.* That had to hurt, but he didn't leave the ministry. Jesus was in the house ministering while his mother stood outside. They came to Him and told Him his mother was outside. Jesus said, *Who is my mother, except them that do the will of God.* That had to hurt, but she never left his ministry. Remember, loyalty is proven when you get hurt in ministry, but you learn how to manage the hurt, bounce back from the hurt and continue to be a great help in ministry.

I finished up the last chapter by telling you to push past the pain. The reason it's important to push past the pain is because there's something more important on the other side of the pain. There's purpose, there's a plan, and an impartation of the anointing on the other side of the pain. I've had to sit people down. I know that had to hurt, but some are still with me. I've had to address people's sin publicly. I know that had to hurt, but some are still with me. I've had to let staff go. I know that had to hurt, but some are still with me. I've had to tell people, "No. The church can't pay your car note." I know that had to hurt, but some are still with me. I've had to set parameters for people. I know that had to hurt, but some are still with me.

I'm not saying I was wrong. All I'm saying is that they were hurt, but some of my best members are the members who have been hurt, but are still with me. Loyalty is proven when you get hurt in ministry, but you learn how to handle the hurt because deep down you know it wasn't meant to hurt you. The hurt was meant to help you. The hurt can make you bitter or the hurt can make you better. It depends on how well you manage the test.

CHAPTER 5

The Loyalty of God

Hebrews 6:13-18

For when God made promise to Abraham, because he could swear by no greater, he sware by himself, 14 Saying, Surely blessing I will bless thee, and multiplying I will multiply thee. 15 And so, after he had patiently endured, he obtained the promise. 16 For men verily swear by the greater: and an oath for confirmation is to them an end of all strife. 17 Wherein God, willing more abundantly to shew unto the heirs of promise the immutability of his counsel, confirmed it by an oath: 18 That by two immutable things, in which it was impossible for God to lie, we might have a strong consolation, who have fled for refuge to lay hold upon the hope set before us:

Remember we're talking about the Law of Loyalty. In this passage of scripture, we see three words that reference the legal system or the law: 1. Swear, 2. Oath, 3. Counsel.

The first term "swear" is mentioned in verse 13. *For when God made promise to Abraham, because he could swear by no greater, he sware by himself.* To swear is to affirm truth. In a court of law, when you give testimony the clerk asks you to place your left hand on the Bible, raise your right hand and then asks, "Do you swear to tell the truth, the whole truth, and nothing but the truth, so help you God?"

The second term "oath" is mentioned in verse 16. "*For men verily swear by the greater, and an oath for confirmation is to them an end of all strife.*" Remember growing up when there was strife between two people as to who was telling the truth or not? One would say, "Swear on your grandmomma's grave then!" That was swearing by the greater. And if one person swore, it suggested that he or she must be telling the truth and it put an end to all strife. Because God had no one greater to swear by, He swore by himself. God doesn't have a mother or a father or a grandparent to swear by so the Bible says He swore by himself. In other words, He was saying "I swear to God I'm going to bless you Abraham."

The third term "counsel" is mentioned in verse 17. It talks about the immutability of His counsel, which is a term often used in a court of law. It means advice given especially in a legal matter. In other words, the covenant (contract) that God cut with Abraham was a legal matter, and his counsel to Abraham in this matter was: *Surely blessing I will bless thee, and multiplying I will multiply thee.* And his counsel to you is: *If ye be Christ's then are ye Abraham's seed and heirs according to the promise.*

Now you know why He's called Wonderful Counselor. God is faithful (loyal) to bring His promises to pass in your life. Let's look at some ways that God's loyalty manifests in our lives.

Hebrews 13:5 (Amplified Bible)

Let your character or moral disposition be free from love of money [including greed, avarice, lust, and craving for earthly possessions] and be satisfied with your present [circumstances and with what you have]; for He [God] Himself has said, I will not in any way fail you nor give you up nor leave you without support. [I will] not, [I will] not, [I will] not in any degree leave you helpless nor forsake nor let [you] down (relax My hold on you)! Assuredly not!]

1. The loyalty of God will never leave you.

The psalmist said *when my father and my mother forsake me, then the Lord will take me up.* God told Moses *my presence shall go with thee.* David said *though I walk through the valley of the shadow of death, I will fear no evil, for thou art with me.* Single parents, you're not raising your children alone. God is with you! You're not going through any attacks by yourself. God is with you! Your man/woman may have left you, but God is with you! You may be facing a legal situation right now, but God is with you!

David said *surely goodness and mercy shall follow me all the days of my life.* Whether you were going through problems with your teenager, a divorce, chemotherapy, surgery, or bankruptcy God was with you! The loyalty of God will never leave you.

Psalm 91:11 (Amplified Bible)

For He will give His angels [especial] charge over you to accompany and defend and preserve you in all your ways [of obedience and service].

2. The loyalty of God will always defend you.

Remember when satan said to God concerning Job, I can't touch him because of the hedge of protection you have around him? God was defending Job. Remember when the Israelites put blood over the doorposts so the death angel couldn't destroy Israel? God was defending them. Remember when they brought the woman caught in adultery to Jesus? Jesus didn't condemn her; he defended her. The loyalty of God will always defend you.

Loyalty is not just informing a person; loyalty is defending a person. Let me explain. If a person comes to me with a mouthful of negative things that someone else has said about me, it informs me but the fact that the person gathered so much information suggests that the person didn't defend me. If someone said something about your mother or your child, you wouldn't just inform them, you would defend them. You would go old school and put your hair up in a ponytail, take your earrings off, kick off your shoes, put some Vaseline on your face and say, "Let's do this."

That's how adamant God is about defending you as His child. No weapon formed against you shall prosper and every tongue that rises against you shall be condemned. In the movie a *Few Good Men*, Captain Ross said "I represent the government of the United States without passion or prejudice." The devil is the accuser of the brethren, but God is your defense attorney, and God represents you without passion or prejudice. It doesn't matter how you messed up. It doesn't matter that you made mistakes. It doesn't even matter that you're guilty, God defends you. We sing a song at our church that says: Jesus precious Jesus defender of my soul/Lord you rule in justice/You're my hero. The loyalty of God will always defend you.

Psalm 37:25

I have been young, and now am old; yet have I not seen the righteous forsaken, nor his seed begging bread.

3. The loyalty of God faithfully provides for you.

David said I've been young and now I'm old. This statement suggests that through every season, stage and situation He had watched God faithfully provide for the righteous. Isn't it amazing how through every season, stage and situation of your life God has provided faithfully?

My wife's parents divorced when she was three years old, and I'll never forget her telling me that, without having to go through the court system, her mother would go to the mailbox monthly, and faithfully receive money from my wife's father. She never received a letter that said, "Sorry. Times are tough right now maybe next month." She said her mother received the money faithfully every month. If an earthly father can be that faithful, how much more faithful is our heavenly father? Let me serve as God's mailman and tell you that the money, the provision and the resources are in the mail. The loyalty of God faithfully provides for you!

CHAPTER 6

Paths, Places, & People

Ruth 1:15-16 *And she said, Behold, thy sister in law is gone back unto her people, and unto her gods: return thou after thy sister in law. 16 And Ruth said, Intreat me not to leave thee, or to return from following after thee: for whither thou goest, I will go; and where thou lodgest, I will lodge: thy people shall be my people, and thy God my God:*

We often talk about how Ruth was loyal to Naomi, but let's break it down and look at three specific areas that Ruth was loyal to.

Ruth said *for whither thou goest, I will go.* She was loyal to the path.

1. Be loyal to the paths that God takes you.

Every person has a particular path that leads them to their purpose. Scripture is full of paths. Psalm 16:11 says *Thou wilt shew me the path of life.* Psalm 23:3 *says He restoreth my soul: he leadeth me in the paths of righteousness for his name's sake.* Psalm 119:105 says *Thy word is a lamp unto my feet, and a light unto my path.* Proverbs 3:5, 6 says *Trust in the Lord with all thine heart; and lean not unto thine own understanding. In all thy ways acknowledge him, and he shall direct thy paths.* Be loyal to the paths that God takes you.

I remember when I was a kid we would walk to the playground. Instead of walking to the corner to get there, we would create our own path. We would cut through someone's yard – taking a shortcut, bypassing the process. There are no shortcuts to success and you cannot bypass the process to God's promises. You have to stay loyal to the path that God takes you.

In the neighborhood that I live in, there is only one way in and one way out. We often want another path to get to where we're going, but sometimes there's only one way to your divine destination and you have to stay loyal to the path that God takes you. Once I was leaving a pastors' retreat late at night out in the country and the roads were dark. There were long periods before I would see a sign to let me know that I was on the right road to get home. Sometimes you don't see any signs that you're going in the right direction, but you have to stay loyal to the path that God takes you.

The Law of Loyalty

I remember Central Ohio's blizzard of 1977. I was 13 years old. The snow was so deep it was almost impossible to walk through. I'll never forget finding the footprints that someone who had walked that path before me made, and how as I walked in the person's steps it made my journey easier. God is faithful to supply footprints for you to follow when you're walking through a storm, but you have to stay loyal to the path that God takes you.

One time my family and I were leaving for a vacation, and we drove through a stretch of highway that was filled with potholes. We were expecting to have a good time and enjoy the trip, but on the way we had to deal with potholes. Sometimes an unhappy marriage, an affair, an addiction, picking up weight, or not passing the exam can be a pothole. But can I tell you that God is in the business of paving the potholes in your life. Things are about to be filled up, leveled out and smoothed over, but you have to stay loyal to the path that God takes you.

Ruth said *for whither thou goest, I will go; and where thou lodgest I will lodge.* She was loyal to the place.

2. Be loyal to the places that God sends you.

Acts 7:20

In which time Moses was born, and was exceeding fair, and nourished up in his father's house three months: 21 And when he was cast out, Pharaoh's daughter took him up, and nourished him for her own son. 22 And Moses was learned in all the wisdom of the Egyptians, and was mighty in words and in deeds.

Moses was educated in a civilization unsurpassed by any other nation at that time. His training was designed to prepare him for a high office, or even the throne of Egypt. He became familiar with life in Pharaoh's courts and in Pharaoh's house. He was schooled in the writing and literary ideas of the time. He was educated in Egypt. In other words, I believe Moses was purposely placed in Pharaoh's palace to learn how to lead – not to lead the Egyptians, but to lead the children of Israel. The reason we need to be loyal to the places God sends us is because there are some lessons that God wants us to learn in that particular place.

God said *Go to the ant thy sluggard and be wise.* He sends us to a place to learn a lesson. God told Jeremiah to *go down to the potter's house and observe the work that the potter performs on the wheel.* In other words, He sent him to a place to learn a lesson. God told Abraham to *go to the land of Moriah and offer thy son as a burnt offering.* As Abraham was about to slay his son God stopped him. Abraham learned that obedience is better than sacrifice. Then God told Abraham to look over because He has provided a lamb for the offering and Abraham called the name of that place Jehovah Jireh. He didn't call the place the Spot of My Obedience, Sacrificial Hill, or Offering up My Son; he called the place Jehovah Jireh, which means my provider. What I'm saying is Abraham went to Moriah for one thing, but while he was there he learned another.

Have you ever gone somewhere for one thing, but while you were there you learned something else? You took the job thinking it was for the salary, benefits, and a 401k, but instead you learned it was so you could be trained in customer service, facilitating groups, marketing, computers, streamlining processes, team building, and leadership. You were learning lessons in Pharaoh's house so you could be effective in God's house. People thought they were coming to our church because they were in need, but since they've been here they've learned that God supplies all their needs, God is their source, Jehovah

Jireh is their provider, and God is not trying to take something from them as much as He's trying to get something to them. There are lessons that God wants us to learn in the places He sends us. So it's vital to stay loyal to the places God sends you.

Ruth said *for whither thou goest, I will go; and where thou lodgest, I will lodge: thy people shall be my people.* She was loyal to the people.

3. Be loyal to the people to whom God connects you.

Let's look at three characteristics that Naomi possessed that made Ruth loyal to her.

Conquerors

Naomi was a conqueror in Ruth's life. To conquer means to overcome difficulties. Naomi overcame a famine and the death of her husband and her two sons. She was a strong individual.

You want to stay close to conquerors. The values and virtues that we learn in life are learned by watching someone deal with difficulties and overcome obstacles. I believe Ruth was loyal to Naomi because she admired and desired her strength and her ability to conquer the challenges she faced.

Contributors

Naomi was a contributor in Ruth's life, not a consumer. She took Ruth from the place of famine to the place where there was food. You want to hang around people who feed you – people who feed your spirit, intellect, vision and future. Remember the movie *Little Shop of Horrors?* The plant would yell "Feed me Seymour! Feed me!" You ought to be saying feed me brother! Feed me! Feed me sister! Feed me! Feed me friend! Feed me! Feed me Pastor, feed me. God said *I will give you pastors who will feed thee with knowledge and understanding.* You won't thrive hanging around takers, bleeders, drainers and consumers. Remember these people are subtractors and dividers. You want the people in your life to be adders and multipliers. Be faithful and loyal to the contributors that God puts in your life.

Connectors

Naomi was a connector in Ruth's life. She connected Ruth to a wealthy man named Boaz. Ruth never would have met Boaz if it wasn't for Naomi connecting them.

Sis, you may meet some guy and because he's not the most handsome dude in the world you may act as if he doesn't exist. I'm not saying he's your husband, but he could be the connector to your husband. The only thing keeping you from finding your soul mate is a connection. The only thing keeping your business from growing is a connection. The only thing keeping your company from climbing is a connection – one associate, one friend, one client, one investor can make all the difference. I'm talking about the power of a connector!

The woman at the well connected the city to Jesus when she said, "Come see a man." The chief butler connected Joseph to Pharaoh; Naaman's wife's maid connected Naaman to Elisha. I know the maid may not impress you, but the man that the maid knows might make all the difference in your life! Be loyal to the people to whom God connects you.

CHAPTER 7

Take One for the Team

John 15:12

This is my commandment, That ye love one another, as I have loved you,

13 Greater love hath no man than this, that a man lay down his life for his friends.

As I was reading this passage of scripture one day, it leaped off the page at me. Through it God showed me the expression of loyalty is in taking one for the team. Think back to chapter one when I talked to you about how men pledge their allegiance to their respective gang or to the mafia. Often these men serve as fall guys and go to prison for someone higher up in the organization. That's their way of taking one for the team. It's the same way when a basketball player takes a charge; he's taking one for the team. When a baseball player allows himself to get hit by a pitch to improve his team's chances of winning, he's taking one for the team too. When a guy acts interested in a woman who's not so good looking so that his friends can have an opportunity to get with the women who are good looking, he's taking one for the team. The expression of loyalty is in taking one for the team.

Loyalty is laced with the spirit of selflessness. It is the willingness to sacrifice for the betterment of something else. I believe loyalty is birthed out of love. This is why Jesus said *greater love hath no man than this, that a man lay down his life for his friends.*

I've seen people lay down their life for the things they love. I've seen people stay after work to get the job done even when they were not asked to. I've seen mothers go without a meal so their children can eat. I've seen pastors take their personal money to pay for the needs of the church. These are examples of people making a sacrifice for the betterment of others, or taking one for the team.

In chapter five, I talked about the loyalty of God. God is loyal to you because He loves you. Jesus is the greatest example of sacrifice for the betterment of others, or someone taking one for the team. Think about it. 2 Corinthians 5:21 says for *He hath made him to be sin for us, who knew no sin; that we might be made the righteousness of God in him.* That's taking one for the team. Isaiah 53:5 says *he was wounded for our transgressions, he was bruised for our iniquities: the chastisement of our peace was upon him; and with his stripes we are healed.* That's taking one for the team. 2 Corinthians 8:9 says *For ye know the grace of our Lord Jesus Christ, that, though he was rich, yet for your sakes he became poor, that ye through his poverty might be rich.* That's taking one for the team. Aren't you so glad that the Lord took one for the team?

The people at your workplace are a team. If you have employees, you have a team. If you are a pastor, you lead a team. If you are married, the two of you are a team. If it's just you and your child, you are a team. The Bible says it's not good that man should be alone. That's why God is faithful to put all of us on a team. I believe man operates at his best when he's part of a team. When's the last time you took one for the team?

The 2012 Olympic Games are going on in London, and I love watching them. What I love most is how athletes at the highest level of their sport put everything on the line to win for their country and fight for their team. When the medal winners stand at the podium as their individual flags are being raised, it's a picture perfect display of loyalty. It is a very heartfelt moment, as the tears of joy, success, and fulfillment begin to roll down each athlete's face – not simply for individual achievement but for what they were able to accomplish for their team.

While Olympians have a great love for their country, we as Christians must have a great love for God, the Church, and the Word of God. Out of that love develops a loyalty to put everything on the line to win for the Kingdom and fight for the team.

I started this book by talking to you about the American flag and I'll end on that note. Remember, the federal flag code says the United States flag should be displayed daily on or near the main administration building of every public institution. In other words, displaying the US flag near public institutions is a law, and it is a statement of loyalty to our government. In the sanctuary of our church, we have an American flag, and a Christian flag. Whoever comes into the sanctuary of Kingdom Christian Center Church can see that the Law of Loyalty is in operation concerning our government. But we also have the Christian flag on display, which is our statement of loyalty to the government of God also known as the Kingdom. Every time our partners come to church I want them to see those flags and remember their loyalty and their responsibility to something greater than self and to have a willingness to take one for the team.

Taking one for the team sets the Law of Loyalty in motion. The law of gravity says what goes up must come down. The law of reciprocity says what goes around comes around. The law of seedtime and harvest says the seed is in itself and it reproduces after its own kind. These laws work every single time when you work them. You can't break a law and expect it to work for you.

Like all these laws, the Law of Loyalty will work for you if you work it. This law says loyalty produces loyalty. It says loyalty isn't loyalty, if it isn't put to the test. It says he that is loyal over little will be ruler over much. Make loyalty a part of your everyday life and you will experience the full manifestation of God's blessing.

CHAPTER 8

Inspiring Quotes on Loyalty

O King be loyal to the royal within you.

        -William Shakespeare, English poet

Where the battle rages, there the loyalty of a soldier is proved.

        -Martin Luther, 16th-century theologian

Leadership is a two way street, loyalty up and loyalty down.

>   -Grace Murray Hopper, US Navy officer

Confidentiality is the virtue of the loyal.

>   -Edwin Louis Cole, founder of Christian Men's Network

I'll take 50% efficiency to get 100% loyalty.

>   -Samuel Goldwyn, American film producer

The greater the loyalty of a group toward the group, the greater is the motivation among the members to achieve the goals of the group.

>   -Rensis Likert, organizational psychologist

A friend is someone who walks in the room when everyone else is walking out.

>   -Gary Moore, musician

Better to have one woman on your side than ten men.

> -Robert Jordan, author

The strength of a family, like the strength of an army, is in its loyalty to each other.

> -Mario Puzo, author

A person who deserves my loyalty receives it.

> -Joyce Maynard, author

There is no friend as loyal as a book.

> -Ernest Hemingway, author

Loyalty means nothing unless it has at its heart the absolute principle of self-sacrifice.

> -Woodrow Wilson, 28th President of the United States

The Law of Loyalty

You can buy a person's hands but you can't buy his heart. His heart is where his enthusiasm, his loyalty is.

-Stephen R. Covey, management expert

When we are debating an issue, loyalty means giving me your honest opinion, whether you think I'll like it or not. Disagreement, at this state, stimulates me. But once a decision is made, the debate ends. From that point on, loyalty means executing the decision as if it were your own.

-Colin Powell, former US Secretary of State

The game is my life. It demands loyalty and responsibility, and it gives me back fulfillment and peace.

-Michael Jordan, NBA legend

Loyalty should not require people to compromise their character. True friends will never ask you to behave in a way that is contrary to who you really are.

-Dr. Robyn Silverman, professional speaker

The foundation stones for a balanced success are honesty, character, integrity, faith, love and loyalty.

-Zig Ziglar, motivational speaker

If a man asks me for my loyalty, I will give him my honesty. If a man asks me for my honesty, I will give him my loyalty!

-John Boyd, US Air Force pilot fighter

You don't earn loyalty in a day. You earn loyalty day-by-day.

-Jeffrey Gitomer, business trainer

Respect is earned. Honesty is appreciated. Trust is gained. Loyalty is returned.

- Unknown

Made in the USA
Middletown, DE
23 April 2025